May the moments spent with this book
be filled with freedom of thought, expression, and travel.

Thank you for inspiring pages of this book:
IFC's *Portlandia* & MindfulNest stores in Los Angeles, California.

". . . put a bird on it!"

In celebration of owls, falcons, eagles, and other birds.

COLOR
MAJESTIC BIRDS

© 3 March 2017
Lynnette Rozine Prock
www.**MyDreamsMatter**.com

ISBN-13: 978-1539544074
ISBN-10: 1539544079
(CreateSpace Assigned)

Adult Coloring Books
Kids Coloring Books

ABOUT ROZINE

When I first moved to Los Angeles, I remember having a dream about a home office that didn't exist to me at the time. I saw a fancy computer screen sitting on top of a vintage wooden desk with wrought iron drawer pulls. A yellow sticky note posted on the monitor reminds me of an important message: HAVE FUN! Outside of the open windows in my dream, from the tops of trees in a dense oak and pine forest, I hear owls' hoots echo through the crisp, night air.

Now, years after having that dream, here I sit, writing an introduction on a wireless keyboard while looking at a large, flat-screen monitor. Pretty fancy! A bright yellow post-it note reminds me of an upcoming henna gig that is sure to be a lot of fun for me and the guests attending the party. My beautiful, vintage wooden desk, with stylish iron drawer pulls is surrounded by windows that overlook a dense oak and pine covered hilltop. Often, on crisp, cool nights, owls hoot from the tree tops.

This coloring book honors believing in fantastical dreams, no matter how far from reality they seem to be at the time of inception. Please join my celebration of illustrations by adding color to the black and white outlines of owls and their majestic bird friends.

MY CREATIVE PROCESS:

In case you were wondering, I illustrate, design, and publish all of my books!

I get inspired by a theme around something that intrigues me. In this book's case: birds. I begin by drawing basic bird shapes in pencil. Once I'm satisfied with the primitive outlines, I trace my pencil with Sharpie markers. Then, I make dozens of copies before decorating each page with henna-inspired patterns, (see page 107).

In about a month, I compile between fifty and one hundred bird-themed illustrations. I edit repetitive or erroneous pages until I am satisfied with thirty or so final drawings.

The act of creating coloring books feeds an obsession in a positive and constructive way over an extended period of time. The result is one I can be proud of. Not only because I created something I think is pretty neat, but also because I know that others can also enjoy my efforts.

Imagine if I obsessed negatively or destructively. I would hurt myself and likely those who care for me. I share this story here to encourage anyone in need of a distraction from toxic behavior. Please. . . Color. Draw. Create. Express yourself in a positive, constructive way each and every time negativity attempts to knock at your door. Take note of the end result! You might actually enjoy yourself. I'm betting you do.

5

9

21

23

27

29

33

35

39

45

47

51

61

63

65

69

73

75

83

87

91

101

If you were to draw a bird, what would it look like?
Use this page to sketch some ideas.

Can you write down which pages these pictures are on?

Extra Challenge: Some of these are on more than one page!

Can you count how many times each of these is used throughout the book?

_____   _____   _____

_____   _____   _____

Be sure to check out Rozine's other books:

Live Life For A Living

This inspirational guide encourages you to make a living doing what you love, offering suggestions for being financially sound while pursuing dreams.

My Dreams Matter

This 38-page coloring book and journal is packed full of beautiful reminders of the joy that can be found within us, when we take the time to notice.

Quiet The Mind

This all age, art-therapy activity workbook is filled with tools to help develop self-awareness, like: positive affirmations, journalizing exercises, black and white illustrations for coloring, and even a quirky scavenger hunt.

Energize Your Life

Another all age, art-therapy activity workbook similar to *"Quiet The Mind"* with a focus on physical health and vitality. Positive affirmations are directed at healing physical, emotional, and mental pains.

Know Your Self

One more from the series of all age, art-therapy activity workbooks. *"Know Your Self"* helps build confidence for success. Activities and prompts will help you understand why and how you are unique, leading you to know your true purpose.

Mandala Meditation

Color and draw repetitive mandalas while meditating on suggested thoughts written to match the meaning of the symbolism used in each illustration. Relax, de-stress, and create with this all-age coloring book focused on building self-esteem.

www.Amazon.com/author/rozine

Look for the other books in the COLOR THINGS series:

COLOR SUGAR SKULLS

Both Dia de los Muertos (Day of the Dead) and henna traditions celebrate the magic and mysticism of life. Rozine shares her love of culture by creating over thirty unique sugar skulls decorated with henna patterns.

COLOR SEA LIFE

Rozine celebrates her love of oceans, seas, and waterways with over fifty unique sea life drawings adorned with ancient henna designs. *COLOR SEA LIFE* includes illustrations of fish, seashells, octopi, turtles, and boats.

COLOR MAJESTIC BIRDS

Over fifty different illustrations of flying animals and their homes are honored in this coloring book. Each page features unique henna-inspired patterns and designs.

Connect & Discover More Inspirational Fun:

www.**MyDreamsMatter**.com

twitter.com/**MyDreamsMatter**

youtube.com/**MyDreamsMatter**

facebook.com/**MyDreamsMatter**

pinterest.com/**MyDreamsMatter**

instagram.com/**Rozine3**

zazzle.com/**rozine***

Also published by Lynnette Rozine Prock:

WOW! SOLAR SYSTEM by Candice Starr Lester

Explore our Earth's solar system in this fact-filled coloring book. Learn about planets, stars, moons and space with astronomical exercises, activities, and illustrations.

www.ingramcontent.com/pod-product-compliance
Lightning Source LLC
Chambersburg PA
CBHW051945280526
45789CB00009B/3178